Through the Eyes of Evil

by

Chris Fife

© 9/29/2017

Table of Contents

Introduction

I read this book by Christopher Browning called Ordinary Men: Reserve Police Battalion 101 and the Final Solution in Poland. It changed the way I thought about the Holocaust. I was shocked at what I read that ordinary police men who were too old to fight on the World War II front were assigned to go through villages and kill Jews. I was surprised that it was these ordinary men, not Nazis who were killing the Jews during the Holocaust.

I have read about many atrocities since and wondered how normal people could turn into killers almost overnight. It has baffled me through the years as I have studied the subject. Since I teach history and geography it has been part of my preparation for lessons I teach in my class.

This book takes a look at evil in its many forms and how it creeps into the hearts of people everywhere. The book addresses the questions; Why do people commit atrocities? Can anyone turn into a killer? What does it take to do something horrible?

It reminds me of the scene in the Star Wars movie where Anakin Skywalker is debating what to do as the Emperor is asking for his help. Anakin with the fear of losing his wife chooses to help the Emperor. This single act places Anakin on the Emperor's side and the dark side of the force. He then goes around killing several people and children without mercy. Even though this is fiction there is more reality in it than people think. There may not be a dark side, but there is evil in the world. We will explore it and then decide what to do with it.

Chapter One: What is Evil?

There will be those who say evil does not exist. They may claim that people do things that are not detrimental to society and they did it because of some chemical imbalance, abuse as a child, or just learned the behavior through their environment. People would say their is no Devil, Satan, or being that promotes evil. People are not influenced by some unseen force to do wicked acts. There is nothing like witchcraft or people practicing black magic.

Then there are those on the other side of the scale who are constantly fearful of witches or demons stealing their children. They believe there are several groups who practice black magic and human sacrifice. These people live in fear and see evil at every turn. They may even promote the fear saying the world is going to end and everyone is evil.

Lets take a look at these extremes and try to look at somewhat of a middle ground or at least attempt to describe what evil is. You may evil is doing something bad. For one person what they do is not bad and other it is. A teacher may tell a student, "You need to stop talking and sit up straight, you are being bad." The student on the other end thinks that what she is doing is not bad and it is okay to talk and slouch in her chair. There becomes a conflict between the two points of view.

Breaking Laws

Most people would admit that breaking a law is bad. Rosa Parks who sat at the front of the bus because she was tired broke the law. Does that mean Rosa Parks was bad? Of course not. The bus laws were made by racist people. Does it then mean the

the law was bad? Does it mean those who wrote the law and enforced it were evil?

It can be very hard sometimes to judge what is evil and what isn't. People generally do not wake up and tell themselves they are going to be bad for the day. Some do and maybe that makes them evil. A true crime is when someone breaks the law with criminal intent. This means a person willingly breaks the law. The act of breaking the law is done with premeditation. Often the person plans out the crime many days in advance or at least thinks about it before he commits the crime.

Most laws were made by people in order to protect the people from harm. Traffic laws are in place to prevent people from getting into a car crash and hurting other people. Yet many people will speed and run a stop sign once in a while. Does that make people who speed evil? There have been terrorists who have used their vehicle to plough through crowds of people with the intent of killing as many people as the terrorist can. Are these people evil?

Laws often originated from religious laws. The ten commandments has been part of the Christian world in Europe and the Americas as a foundation for the laws of the land. Murder comes from the commandment not to kill. Stealing comes from one of the commandments, and so it a few others. Yet there is no law about observing the Sabbath day in most countries. There is no law about committing adultery. So it seems like countries and people pick and choose what to make as laws of the land, and will often pick which ones to follow.

You might speed on the freeway, but would never steal or kill anyone. Many of the laws are split into felonies and misdemeanors. The felonies include theft and murder. The misdemeanors include the traffic laws and other minor laws. So is it okay to obey felony laws and then choose which minor law to keep.

Breaking laws is one indicator that a person may be heading down a road that is paved with evil intentions. A person with a criminal record tends to do more bad things than a person without a criminal record. There are many exceptions to this as people start to break minor laws and then larger ones. One broken law may lead to another broken law.

How You Treat Your Neighbor

How a person treats his neighbor may be an indicator as to the evil or good in a person. If you follow the golden rule taught by Jesus you will be kind and caring towards your neighbor. Others may treat their neighbor as an enemy or a victim. The intent to do good and serve or the intent to harm and take advantage can show what is happening.

It is interesting how a woman may marry an abusive man having seen the way he treats others. He becomes the abusive husband and she becomes the victim in the marriage. She enables the behavior and he thinks that his behavior is okay. If she would have just thought about his behavior before ether had gotten married she would have been saved a lot of pain and suffering.

There are situations when someone cannot help the situation they are in. This is where evil plays out and the true nature is reveals as one person takes advantage of another through abuse and neglect. The worst is when a parent takes things out on a child, or they simply treat the child with ill intent. Evil could be considered how people treat each other. If they harm others they may be doing things that are evil.

The first step in recognizing evil is how a person treats another person. You might take a look at how those of the Nazi party in Germany during World War II were evil because they killed so many Jews. Yet before the war and the Holocaust people lives and worked together without bloodshed. Things also returned to normal after the war as families came together.

What Evil is Not

Evil is not a refugee who is fleeing her country because of war. She is taking her three children to another country for safety. It is not a person who is practicing his religion. He is just doing what he believes in. It is not someone who has a different political view than you.

Evil is not a child that makes a mistake, because she hasn't been taught that what she is doing is wrong. It is not having a terrible thought about someone, and then dismissing it. It is not hurting someone and then feeling guilty about it.

Humans make some horrible mistakes sometimes. It is part of learning about life and how to get along with people who have different ideas than you do. There may have been times you did something that was very bad. There are times when you have done things that were good.

The point is that it is important to recognize the good and bad, the right and wrong, the evil and the righteous. Everyone is born innocent and pure. You can see this in the eyes of any infant. Little children are the same. They may do things that are wrong and make mistakes, but they still have an innocence about them. Children are innately good and are not evil. They don't become evil until they are teenagers.

Children are not evil, nature is not evil, animals are not evil, people are not evil, books are not evil, toys are not evil. The list can go on and on. There are a lot of things in this world that are not evil. Therefore we should be more pure than evil.

Pure Evil

Pure evil is something that resides in the dark areas of our brain. It comes from the father of all lies Lucifer, Satan, the son of the morning. He and his followers set in the hearts of people everywhere evil. There is just one purpose or mission of evil.

The goal of evil is to destroy a person's soul. Destruction and misery is the mission of evil. It wins when people are in misery without hope filled with despair. It wins when people are filled with hate and fear. It wins when people find enjoyment in hurting others. It wins when people use their desires to make other people miserable.

Forms of evil can be murder where someone takes the life of another person thus robbing them of happiness and causing misery of the victims loved ones. Rape is another evil act that robs the victim of her dignity and causes despair and suffering. Other acts of violence including fighting, torture, and abuse causes the victims much pain and suffering and will impact their mental health and create fear in many people.

War and the atrocities of war create misery and hopelessness to an entire country or region of the world. It brings about ill intent and revenge as well as the suffering of thousands or millions of people. The evils of slavery are still present in the world today.

Victims of crimes have to suffer because of the consequences associated with the crime. This could be theft, vandalism, or an attack on a person's character. Even the small things like car accidents can create an atmosphere to allow evil thoughts to enter into a person's mind.

Domestic issues can create situations of mistrust, dishonesty, and ill feelings towards each other. Victims of domestic violence, abuse, and neglect often have years of suffering and depression. There is nothing more evil than the act of hurting little children through abuse or neglect.

Chapter Two: The Seeds of Evil

Everyone is born with good and evil in them. Little Children are protected by divine manifestation and often sheltered by parents. It doesn't mean that evil things cannot happen to little children. This is the saddest thing in the world when a little child gets hurt by someone else. It means that little children do not exhibit evil intent. The things they do that are wrong are out of ignorance rather than evil intent.

The seeds of evil start then a child starts to get older and understand more about the world. This could be something the child starts to pick up from her parents or friends. It could be something in the environment that causes her to start to access evil thoughts and emotions. It could even be an event that forces her to move towards the evil in her.

Even thought we all have good and evil within us. We get to choose which one to follow. There may be a time when we may choose to do something wrong, and another time when we choose to do something good. This is generally the normal cycle of life most people go through. Some people choose to do more good in the world, and some choose to do more evil in the world.

Addiction

Evil can be an addictive practice. You probably know of someone who is very negative and is constantly complaining, blaming, and upset about everything. You may also know of someone who is constantly in trouble or getting into trouble. You may know someone who finds pleasure in hurting other people or likes to watch other people get hurt.

Many people enjoy watching fights and violent shows. They may even watch shows where people are hurt through immorality. These things can be highly addictive. Many people will become addicted to a violent video game. They may become addicted to pornography that exploits women and children. They may be addicted to gambling or shopping which leads to going into debt.

Addictions lead to hate, fear, and hopelessness. This is where evil resides. It is something that leads to more evil in a person's life. Addictions causes the destruction of an individual and causes misery and despair to those around the person.

The Human Brain

Evil resides in the primal part of our brain that is often referred to our reptilian part of the brain. It is the area that triggers our survival instincts and has no reasoning attached to it. This primal mind focuses on the pleasure center and seeks to satisfy our most vial desires. Once in the primal area of the brain a person does not think about what is good. The brain simply triggers emotions that will block all levels of reasoning.

This is why people who take drugs or alcohol lose all sense of reasoning. People who are on drugs will kill or hurt someone and feel no remorse over it. They may experience the remorse after they become sober again. But drugs weaken the moral part of the brain where they can understand what is right and what is wrong. Even a drug like marijuana will block the reasoning and thinking area of the brain. People high on marijuana will lose their sense of right and wrong. They will not care about anything including their family and friends.

When something happens to a person to bring about fear adrenaline starts to flow through the body and the prefrontal cortex is blocked which includes reasoning. This is why when people start shouting at each other in an argument it will continue to get worse until a physical altercation results. You can easily fall into the trap if someone is upset with you. They start to yell at you and you start to get upset and before you know it you are throwing a punch at the person.

Evil Creates More Evil

The worse thing about evil is that evil will create more evil. The evil act in one person will create evil intent in another. This is most prevalent in gangs and in areas of the world where there is war. People see friends and relatives get injured or killed and they get this desire to do the same to those who caused this. Violence breeds more violence.

It may start in school with peer pressure or bullying. At first a child feels what he is doing is wrong, but all of the other children are doing it, so he rationalized doing it to belong with the crowd. Then he stops feeling that it is wrong and thinks it is okay to do. Many children who bully other children were bullied themselves, or feel insecure or fearful of others. There is something that triggered the child to bully others. It could be that the child sees his parents bullying others and feels it is the right thing to do.

Social media is a breading ground for good and evil. The evil is the bullying that happens which spreads like wildfire with friends continuing the rumors or acts of terror all in the name of having fun hurting others. One girl may see a hurtful comment by another girl and then retaliate by posting a hurtful comment against the other girl. It becomes a cycle of evil that has destructive consequences. It really doesn't matter who started it all, it matters where it stops.

The cycle of evil can spread like wildfire when people get into a mob mindset. This has happened in neighborhoods with riots. It has happened in schools with gangs. It continues to happen around the world with terrorist groups. People get caught up in the evil of fear, hate, or simply following the energy of the crowd.

The brain gets pumped up with adrenaline and you just want to take action. If you are with a bunch of people smashing things and hurting people the adrenaline or evil inside of you will push you to do the same things as those around you, regardless of what they are doing.

You just have to go to a sporting event and observe how the players and fans react to what it going on. It can be very brutal when people start to get upset in a stadium with thousands watching a game. Players, coaches, and fans will do terrible things to other people because of a silly bad call by a referee, or a cheap shot by a player. They forget that it is just a game. People have gotten seriously hurt because of others getting caught up in the heat of an argument over something silly happening in the game. This is the essence of evil and how it manifests itself throughout the world.

Chapter Three: Ordinary People

So who is evil? Certainly people like Hitler, Stalin, and Charles Manson are evil. Would you believe many ordinary people can be evil as well. I got a calling at my church to teach a Sunday school class. The other teacher I was suppose to teach with was an older person who was just about the kindest warmest person you could meet. Her and her husband were very good people, with no evil in their bones.

It shocked me to learn that her son had shot and killed his ex-wife and mother-in-law. It was unheard of to know these kindhearted people and know one of their children could have done such a thing. There are many people who end up committing very evil things who are average normal people. It is like something snaps inside and they go crazy.

Traumatic Events

In the case of the son who killed his ex-wife, it is a classic example of a man losing it because his wife dumped him. There are a lot of examples where couples have a falling out and one or both go temporary insane over the situation. They allow evil thoughts to come to the surface because of the pain they are having and then act on those evil thoughts. There have been many evil acts committed in the name of love or the breaking of one's heart. Just look at Cleopatra and Mark Anthony who both committed suicide like how Romeo and Juliet did. They simply lost it over what they thought was an overpowering sense of love.

I am not sure that it was actually love or something more sinister at work in their minds. The brain can work in mysterious ways as people have stress and go through sometime simple events to horrifying events. It is strange how one person can handle a situation and another person goes crazy. It could be the chemical makeup in the brain or just the idea that the person at the time allowed the evil thoughts to take control of his mind.

Whenever a person goes through a traumatic event he will start to have powerful feelings and some evil thoughts will surface in the mind. These feelings of fear can turn into hate or rage. One person may continue to escalate the emotions while another person is able to recognize what is happening and force them down as he calms down and starts to analyze the situation.

There can be a stress point where a person just cannot take it anymore. For some people this tress point is higher than others. I have seen teachers get a job and quit after a week at work. Then there are teachers who work for more than 30 years without the stress bothering them. It may be part of how the person is prepared, or it may be how the person deals with the stress.

I can feel it when the stress is getting to me and when I am about to explode. I can feel the anger building inside and there have been times when I have allowed the anger to control my actions, but I still have a little level of control when I do explode. Part of this is that I have learned never to cross a certain line. I do not swear and have never picked up the habit, so when I get angry I do not swear. I may scream, but it is done without vulgarity or done in a demeaning way. But it still frightens me when I get to the point where I am screaming.

So when I do get to the point when I am starting to get angry, I back off and allow myself to calm down. This might mean that I remove myself from the situation. It may mean I remove a student from my classroom. But if I do a dance with may emotions, I will not win the battle. I have worked hard over the years to control my temper and to never cross a line that I have made for myself. This has worked for me so far.

I also do not have any guns in the house and will never own a gun. I do not trust myself around guns, not that I would ever think about using one against anyone unless it was to defend my family. But that I do not believe in guns, and know that if I did ever get to a point where I was very depressed or a traumatic event happened that I could not handle the gun would present itself as an easy escape from the pain.

You can see how good normal people can do evil things when they go through traumatic events and at the time see no way out. I do not know what I would do if something happened to my family especially if it was done by someone else in a criminal manner. I also do not know what would happen if someone robbed me and took everything I own. These situations could trigger me to do something I would not normally do.

Addictions

Normal people will also do evil things when they are addicted to something. Drugs cause people to do very horrible things, because they are trapped in this endless hell of addiction they do not know how to get out. People who are addicted will lie, cheat, steal, and even kill in order to continue the addiction. Bad things often happen to people who are addicted and they end up causing bad things to happen to other people they know.

I know several people who talk about how their mother or father was an alcoholic and how they did evil things to their families. I have read stories how soldiers in order to kill innocent people took drugs or got drunk before killing the people. No matter what the addiction is evil thoughts come into a person's mind in order to rationalize the behavior, keep the behavior a secret, or try to get other people to do the behavior in order to have friends doing what they are doing.

Chemical substances can turn people into monsters, bringing out the evil tendencies they normal suppress. There is a level of resistance we are born with. This is a sense of right and wrong that tells us that we should not do something. This sense of right and wrong helps us to resist evil thoughts so that we do not allow those thoughts to turn into actions. Over the years people may build up this resistance and have more of a clear understanding of what is right and what is wrong. It can be things like drugs that will break down this resistance and cause people to act upon those evil thoughts.

Mob Mentality

I have seen good kids do horrible things at the school I teach at. The reason for this is that they get caught up in the mob mentality where their friends and other kids they know start to do something and then soon everyone is doing it. A minor altercation between two children can turn into a riot in an instant.

There was the riot that took place with the Rodney King trial in Los Angeles. People took to the streets and destroyed their neighborhoods. It was insane what they did and I am certain many of them were average people. It was just that they got caught up with the madness.

The same thing has happened after a professional game where a team won a championship. They get all excited and decide to start destroying things. It is this excitement or adrenaline rush that causes people to get caught up in the moment and do things they would not normally do. The bad thing about the mob mentality is that the people believe that if they join the crowd that their is no consequences and they can get away with whatever they do. The problem with this is that they have to live with what they had done for the rest of their lives.

Mobs are really hard to stop once they get started. They may start as an innocent rally or protest and soon turn into a riot which turns into a civil war. In some cases this may be justified to a certain extent if the government is abusing the people. But it can easily be started by an evil idea which spreads throughout the entire country. There have been several brutal dictators who have been placed into power from a group that started as a mob.

Gangs

You may not think of a member of a gang as an average person. But at one point the child was just a child. Then one day the child was pushed into joining a gang. The gang mentality is based on violence and criminal activity. Organized crime has existed since the dawn of time. It became glamorized during the 1920s and 1930s with Al Capone. Then all kinds of gangs sprung up with drugs as a means to earn money and violence as a means of controlling their territory. Belonging to a gang is a kind of brain washing that changes the mentality of a child into acting on his primal or evil thoughts.

Their idea of respect is through violence and intimidation. It all starts went a child is jumped into the gang. This is done when the child is beaten up by all of the members of the gang sometimes ending up in a hospital. Often the child has siblings, parents, or other relatives who are also members of the gang. It becomes this cycle of gang membership and mentality that exists for generations. Thus they build up a mentality that it is okay to hurt other people, especially if they hurt or disrespect you.

It is interesting to see how members of a gang act as if they are the center of the universe and everything revolves around them and if someone doesn't bow down to them they lash out against them and the rest of the members join in like a nest of hornets. Gang rivalries can last for years with many members killing each other.

They allow their hate, fear, and resentments to take control over their thoughts. There is also drug use involved which compounds the problem. In their eyes what they are doing is not wrong, it is just a part of life. It becomes extremely hard to change the way they think because of how long they have allowed those evil thoughts to control their minds.

It is really sad to think that many of these gang bangers are just kids who could grow up to be great people. Normal children twisted by the evil ideas of a gang. This same process of recruiting children to become monsters has occurred throughout the world. It happens when children are kidnapped and forced into slave labor. It happens when children are forced to become soldiers in a war. It happens when children are indoctrinated to become terrorists. The same mentality exists.

The children are brainwashed where their resistance to evil thoughts and actions are broken down. They may be forced to commit something unthinkable like killing a parent or friend. They are given drugs to take. They are forced to watch terrible things. They are taught to feed upon their hate, their fear, and to use those emotions to become violent and to take action on the evil thoughts in their minds. These children again could grow up to be normal people, but are trained to become killers.

Moral Decay and Taboos

In some societies of the past it was traditional to go to war with a rival tribe and to eat the warriors you killed in battle. Today this is absurd, no one believes cannibalism is okay. Yet in the past in certain areas of the world it was tradition and no one thought about questioning it until another group of people came through and told them it was not okay.

There are evils in the world that had been done in the past and recognized as being evil and are no longer done today. Slavery was one such evil that was widely practiced in the United States and throughout Africa and Europe. It was commonly accepted as a means of making money. Many average people owned slaves. George Washington and Thomas Jefferson owned several slaves. Many of the so called normal people at the time owned slaves which would be considered one of the most evil acts ever.

Slavery was a common practice throughout the ages in Greece and in Rome. In Africa many kingdoms would capture people from each other and sell them as slaves. In the Americas tribes would take people in battle and even adopt them into their own tribes. Sacagawea was captures by a different tribe and sold to a French trapper to be his wife. They later met Lewis and Clark and she ended up being apart of history.

Today there is still slavery, but in general the world has accepted that it is an evil and has made several laws against it. It has forced the world to take a look at human rights and universal rights for everyone.

There are a lot of things in the world that are done as tradition or an acceptable norm, that many people would consider evil. The practice of forbidding girls to attend school could be one. The oppression of women in several countries, and cruelty to animals is another. Yet in some areas of the world these things are part of their culture.

All you have to do is to watch television shows from fifty years ago and then each decade to see what has changed. Smoking was common, until the evils of smoking was revealed and how many people were dying from it. Now it is not as common and many parts of the world have made laws to restrict its use. Television shows and movies have eliminated a lot of characters from smoking, and even make fun at the idea that a lot of people used to smoke.

Yet fifty years ago there were certain ideals about sexuality, language, and respect that were part of the culture. Now in the media those things have reversed so that it is not evil to cheat on your spouse or say unkind things to someone else. Children are growing up with a mixed idea of what is right and what is wrong. Evils of the past are now being accepted as normal behavior.

Ordinary people will do things that are evil, because society says it is okay. They see it done in the movies and the internet so therefore it is okay to do. They may think it is okay because a law is passed saying it is okay. Everyone is doing it so therefore it is okay to do. Right and wrong is no longer black and white. There is a lot of grey in the world, and with this a lot of people are allowing those evil thoughts turn into action. The problem with this is that someone will come along and allow those thoughts turn into ideas and those ideas actions and convince millions of other people to go along with it. I am talking about Hitler, Stalin, and many others in the past who did just that.

Chapter Four: Historic Evil

There are many examples throughout history that illustrate the evil acts of people. Remember at one point many of these people who had committed these acts were normal people. Many of them were caught up in the moment and were seduced by evil intentions. The seeds of evil have been planted in the heart of people for a very long time and they will continue to be planted in the future unless we do something about it. Hopefully we can learn from the lessons from the past.

The historical examples listed are by no means an extensive example. There are volumes written by each and many other books written about other evils that took place. History can give us a picture into the hearts of people influenced by evil intentions.

Cain and Able

Adam and Eve the first parents of humanity had two boys, Cain and Able. Able was a herder of sheep and Cain was a farmer and planted crops. One day Satan came to Cain and told him to offer up a sacrifice to the Lord. This Cain did, but the sacrifice was not accepted. His brother Able's sacrifice was accepted and this made Cain really angry and ended up killing his brother. This would be considered the first murder to have happened.

Cain further rebelled against his family and left to start his own people away from that of his family. The study of the story of Cain and Able show how jealousy and revenge can bring able murder. This drew a line between the rest of Adam and Eves children and Cain and his children.

Jewish Journey

This journey has been documented throughout history in scriptures and historical documents. It is a journey that started long before Christ and thousands of years before the Holocaust. The journey starts with the children of Israel or the Hebrews in Egypt who were the descendants of Israel and Joseph. They were under bondage by the Egyptians. The Egyptians had welcomed Jacob (Israel) and his family with Joseph as a leader in Egypt. But over many years the people forgot about Joseph and thought it would be a good idea to make the Hebrews slaves.

They were slaves for a very long time until Moses came along and helped to lead them to freedom. From there they wondered in the wilderness and finally went to their promised land over the across the river Jordan where they slaughtered the people living their and took the land. This they did according to the word of God. The people in the area were just as bad as they would slaughter other tribal groups all around. The Hebrews were given the law of the the ten commandments and then built their own kingdom of Israel and had several kings the greatest being David.

They were beaten up several times after David and split into two separate kingdoms of Judah and Israel. The majority were taken captive to Babylon when they invaded and many cities destroyed. Then it was the King of Persia who was tricked by one of his leaders to order the death of all of the Jews. It was the faith of Esther who married the king who prevented this from happening. Then Rome came in and took over. Rome destroyed Jerusalem and killed several Jewish people around 70 CE.

The destruction of Israel by the Romans was so complete that people were starving to death and resorted to cannibalism. Many of the Jews were taken to several parts of Europe where they remained to modern times. Judah became Palestine and the Palestinians became the permanent residents.

Jewish people were persecuted throughout Europe including the Spanish inquisition in the 1400s where many were expelled from the country, tortured and killed. There was the Pograms in Russia where many Jewish villages were cleared and Jewish people were forced to live in other areas or forced to leave the country. These Pograms happened around 1900 before World War I. The movie Fiddler on the Roof tells the story about what happened.

So when Hitler came along the seeds of hatred and fear of the Jews had already been planted. Many stereotypes and myths were circling around Europe. The Jewish people were in many countries of Europe and were part of society working, going to school, and serving their country. Many fought for Germany during World War I and many were born and served as faithful German citizens. They same goes for Jewish people in other countries. Jewish people were a minority in Germany as well as other countries in Europe. They would generally keep to themselves and would often marry other Jewish people, but there was intermarrying going on. It is even suggested that Hitler had Jewish ancestry. DNA evidence suggests that he had Jewish blood running through his veins.

The Holocaust was the mastermind of Hitler and several of his Nazi leaders. It was interesting how Hitler who was a failure at art, and was wounded in World War I became the leader of Germany. He even tried to attempt to overthrow the government and was thrown in jail for treason. It was while he was in jail

that he wrote his Mein Kampf which was somewhat of
an autobiography and part of his plans for Germany.
He helped to start the Nazi party which took power
and help Hitler become the leader.

Germany had been blamed for starting World
War I and had to pay war reparations. This made
Germany sink into a bad economic depression and
caused panic throughout the streets. The people
wanted order and Germany to become great again.
Hitler promised all of this. The people believed him
and he took over. He did change things around for the
benefit of Germany, but he also had to have a
scapegoat for all of the problems. The Jews were the
perfect scapegoat.

Hitler also believed in a super race of people
which did not include the Jews. They first made laws
against the Jews where people could not marry a Jew
that was not Jewish, and allowed a lot of retaliation
against the Jewish people to take place. Then many
of the Jewish people lost their businesses and jobs,
then they were rounded up and put into internment
camps and ghettos. It was at this time Hitler came up
with the final solution which was the extermination of
all Jewish people.

It was not just the Jewish people who suffered.
Anyone including mentally disable people and
handicap people were targets. Including soldiers who
were injured in the line of duty to their country. Many
people ended up dying in order to purify the country
and the race of people. Many of the Nazis were
obsessed with the idea. They then would send their
propaganda machine everywhere telling people of the
evils of Jews and how they needed to be stopped.

It was not just the Nazis who killed the Jews
many average people in Eastern Europe either
participated in the act or chose to look the other way

as their neighbors were rounded up and taken to a mass grave where they were shot in the back of the head. The police force that was called up to do the evil act, felt it was their duty to do it, despite not having anything against the people and in many cases thought they were good people. Many got drunk before hand in order to do it, or rationalized that they were sending the people to a better life. Some did go crazy from committing such terrible acts of violence on old men, women, and children.

Why would the Nazis conduct the Holocaust and death camps? Many of them became sadistic animals as they went about the work of death. It was how they continued to twist their minds into something that was not human. Some believed they were at war with the Jews and it was just an act of war. Others just followed orders and felt that it was just part of their duty to their country. Then there were those who genuinely hated Jewish people or those who took out all of their frustrations for the war and the stress out on the Jews.

So how could average people take part in the killings and allow it to happen. Some were afraid to stand up against the Nazis and new what they were capable of with the destruction of their country. There were those who also had ill feelings for the Jews. Many of them thought that if the Germans were occupied with killing the Jews they would not start targeting them. Again it could have been the mob mentality of going along with the crowd.

Many German women and doctors were involved in the Holocaust. There were nurses who would starve infants or poison them. Wives of SS officers were just as brutal to the Jews as their husbands were. When asked about it after the war they simply said it was part of their duty. They had allowed the evil seeds to be planted into their hearts and without remorse or sense of right or wrong too the lives of millions of innocent people.

The Holocaust has been the subject of many books and movies since it happened. In part to help us remember just how low we can go and to prevent something like this from happening again. It was also something that was done by so called civilized people who were supposed to be intelligent.

There was a bright light of millions of Jews who were able to leave and go to other countries to be safe including Albert Einstein. There were those who were rescued by many people throughout Europe, and then there were the Jewish survivors of the camps who were rescued at the end of the war. These people saw the humanity in helping the Jewish people while some of their neighbors did not or even took place.

It must have been very difficult for the people to have gotten along after the war knowing their neighbors did nothing or even took part in the atrocity. Those who did take part, probably had ill feelings for those they knew who helped save the Jews. It was a very difficult time for everyone all over the world trying to recover from the war as well as trying to make things right with the Jewish people. This is why Israel was established in Palestine as a sovereign nation.

Jewish people since the Holocaust have still faced persecution, anti-semitism, and war in Israel. They have fought to survive in a region where their neighbors have tried to defeat Israel several times. You can see how people living in Israel both Jew and Muslim can feed on the seeds of hate, fear, and revenge as Jews try to hold on to Israel and Palestinians try to get their country back.

Armenian Genocide

The Armenian people lived in Turkey. They have a rich culture. Many of them are Christian. This and their distinct culture set them apart from the Turks. So the Turks would persecute and abuse them. During World War I the Turks saw an opportunity to get rid of the Armenians. They removed them from their homes and villages and many of them were slaughtered in the wilderness. There was hundreds of thousands of Armenians who were killed by the officials of Turkey. Many of the Armenians were able to escape the genocide to other countries and they were able to create their own country.

Today the Armenians thrive as a culture. The movie The Promise goes into detail about what happened to the Armenian people. This again happened as evil seeds were planted in the hearts of many of the Turks. The idea of getting ride of a people did not start with Hitler. It was something that has continued throughout history in various parts of the world.

American Indians and Australian Aborigines

In Australia they had a policy where they would take young Aboriginal girls from their homes and put them in a boarding school. They would then marry them off to a white man so that their children would be half white. So eventually the Aboriginal race would be bred out of Australia.

Throughout its history the Aborigines where treated unfairly and hunted down. In the movie Quigley Down Under it portrays how some of the Australians treated the Aborigines. It was a terrible time for Australians. Even today many Aborigines are out of work and there is still some racism going on.

The American Indians have been treated no better. The United States passed a law the Indian Removal Act of 1830 to get rid of the Indians in the East to a land West in what is now Oklahoma. The Cherokee even took their case before the Supreme Court and won. But President Jackson and local leaders refused to accept the decision of the Supreme Court. They were forced out of their homes to resettle in the West. Many of them died along the way. It is known as the Trail of Tears.

There were several massacres that took place against the American Indians. These often involved entire villages of men, women, and children. The genocide that took place consisted of trying to kill all of the bison the plains Indians relied on for food and shelter. It also consisted of trying to kill all of the mustangs that the plains Indians used to hunt with. Biological warfare was also used in order to wipe out the American Indian. Millions died from such diseases as measles and small pox. They would send blankets to a village that had small pox on them and in a matter of weeks almost everyone would be dead. It is hard to believe just how bad it was for a government and people to try to eliminate other humans.

We are not talking about one group of people. We are talking hundreds of distinct cultures and nations who were under attack by the United States government. There were a lot more American Indians five hundred years ago than there are today, and many of the tribes have long since been erased from history.

Why did the European settlers attempt to kill off all of the American Indians? It is as simple as the evil seed of greed and a clash of cultures. The American

Indian way of life was so much different than the Europeans that the Europeans feared them and thought of them as demons. The Europeans also wanted land and all of the resources that went with it. In order to get the land they needed to get ride of the people who lived on the land. This is one reason why when gold was discovered the people who lived their were cleared so that the Europeans could come in and claim it.

Religious Intolerance

Religious intolerance and persecution has occurred since the beginning. We have already taken a look at the Jewish journey. In the past the normal way of doing things was to get rid of those who did not believe as you did so that they would not corrupt you or your children. The Muslims went through the middle east getting rid of all those who would not accept Islam. They left a few unbelievers and forced them to pay taxes and pay tribute to the Islamic leaders.

Christianity became the state religion of Rome and the Roman Empire. It forced everyone to accept the religion. This lead to laws being passed that were religious in nature, and those who disobeyed the laws were subject to punishment and torture by the church. In some case like Joan of Arch people were burned at the stake or executed. There were several people throughout Europe who were put in prison or executed for spreading ideas that were not in line with church doctrine. Many of the women who were killed for witchcraft were probably just outspoken women who said something different than what their priests had said. Scientists and philosophers were also targeted for their ideas and often punished.

Martin Luther who opposed church practice was tried by the church and excommunicated. He would have been killed if it wasn't for some influential nobles in Germany at the time. The Lutheran church was then established and the protestant movement was started. Throughout Europe several people rebelled against the Catholic church and started their own churches. Despite the spread of protestantism throughout Europe there was still a lot of intolerance and many people were persecuted.

Many people sought to come to America for religious freedom. Many found it in the New World. But a lot of the protestant religionists continued to be intolerant of other religions. Many Quakers, Catholics, and other religions were persecuted. Some were tortured and even executed for their beliefs. There was no true religious freedom and even when the Constitution of the United States and the Bill of Rights was accepted religious intolerance was still happening. Many religions fought each other for converts and spread evil lies about other religions.

When the Church of Jesus Christ of Latter-day Saints (Mormons) was established they were persecuted and driven from their homes in four states. One state the governor Wilburn Boggs issued an extermination order to have the Mormons driven from the state or exterminated. This led to several of the Mormons being killed and many more dying in their exodus. The leader of the church Joseph Smith and his brother were killed in Illinois years later and the members of the church were forced to leave once more and went to settle in what is now Utah.

Even today there are people who attack other religions. They are not tolerant of other religions and want to get rid of people who have different beliefs than they do. It is something that has in it seeds of evil thoughts about the fear of something they do not understand. Religious intolerance is at the heart of many of the conflicts and wars that exist today.

Cambodia

The Communist Khmer Rouge under the leadership of Pol Pot went cleansing the country of anyone they thought was a threat to them. In total there were over a million people who were killed and buried in some 20,000 mass graves throughout the country.

The people who were not killed where taken and put to work in state run farms. This terror in the country lasted from 1975-1979. It ended when Vietnam invaded the country and took charge of the government. The country had gone through a civil war before the Khmer Rouge took over, and then they turned the country upside down. The seeds of evil was planted in the hearts of many of the people who belonged to the Khmer Rouge. They are still having trials on people who were involved for crimes against humanity.

Slavery

The evil acts of slavery started when a person was captured or sold into slavery sometimes by parents who had to pay a debt. The person then was hauled off tied together or put in chains with several other people. They were treated like animals as they went to a port in West Africa and left in a dungeon until a slave ship came and stacked them up in the hull of the ship.

The slave ships were so packed with slaves that disease took the lives of a third of the people.

Imagine being on a ship for weeks shackled in one position with urine and excrement filling the place. The smell would be unbearable. People dying all around you. It would be one of the worst tortures imaginable.

Then the people after reaching their destination in the Caribbean or southern states would be sold at auction like cattle. They would then be forced into a life of slavery where they would have to work all day in the fields, get beaten, raped, and dehumanized. If a person started a family the family was often ripped apart as the children were sold to other slave owners. The children never to see their parents again.

These evil actions took place for several hundreds of years involving millions of people. All of this because of greed and the wealth the plantation owners were making. Slavery was big business for Africa, Europe, and the Americas. There were thousands of people who relied on making a money from it. This is why it lasted so long. Greed is one of those seeds of evil that people often have a hard time resisting.

Animal Cruelty

In the past there was a lot of animal cruelty going on. People didn't think anything of it, because they were animals. This involved shows where animals would fight each other including bears, tigers, dogs, and chickens. They would even have people fighting animals. Bull fighting is still something that is practiced in Spain and Mexico.

The conditions in which many animals lived was horrible for the animals being held in small cages with little food and water. This practice was the worst in the circus where wild animals were not allowed to be wild animals and were beaten if they did not do what the trainers wanted them to do.

Animals have been used by people to do work and to entertain people. They did not have any rights and the owners of the animals could do whatever they wanted without any threat of the law.

I remember my drivers education teacher talking about a kid he had gone to school with. He said that he boy treated animals very poorly. My teachers said that the boy ended up in prison. He also said that he could tell that the way he treated animals was the character of the boy. My teacher could tell that the boy already had seeds of evil within him.

How a person treats animals reflects what the person is like. In the teachings of Buddhism and other religions of the East there is a special reverence for life, all life, including animals and insects. If you have ever had a pet or have really paid attention to an animal you can tell that they feel some of the same emotions as we do. They can feel pain and suffering. They can be depressed and they can be happy. Just observe how a dog wags its tail, or a cat runs up and brushed up against its owner. You can also tell when an animal is distressed.

War Atrocities

When it comes to war, the soldiers have committed horrific acts. It got so bad in war time that countries actually got together and came up with some rules. Countries are suppose to abide by those rules, but when you have a war going on, it is difficult to control the soldiers. No one can imagine just how terrible war is and all of the evil that comes from it.

If it wasn't for World War I the second world war would not have happened. Many wars create other wars or ill feelings about groups of people. It becomes an evil cycle of hate and revenge. Not only has there been many genocides that have been hidden inside of wars, there has been women, children, and the elderly who have become victims of war through death, rape, and the loss of loved ones. It often takes decades for a country to recover from a war.

King David

The story of King David is one of tragic loss influenced by evil. First David as a boy defeats Goliath and is ordained by the prophet to be King of Israel. The people love David. Saul who was the King tries to kill him, but ends up dying. David wins many wars and makes Israel a great nation. He is also considered very righteous among his people and the prophet.

Then one day when he should have been away overseeing the war, he remained in the castle and was looking out at night into the village and noticed Bathsheba taking a bath. He lusted after her and had his servants bring her to him. Now David already had several wives. But he allowed lust to get the best of him and slept with a married woman, and did this several times while her husband was away fighting for King David. Bathsheba became pregnant and David tried to cover this up with having her husband come home to be with Bathsheba, only her husband remained in the castle.

David then decided to put Bathsheba's husband in the front of the battle so that he was get killed. Then after Bathsheba's husband was killed the prophet came to him and told David God knew what he had done and would not go unpunished of his

crime. It only took a look and an adulterous
relationship to bring down one of the most powerful
men in the world at the time.

Chapter Five: Modern Evil

You would think that over time people would learn from the mistakes they made in the past. Yet we continually make the same mistakes over and over again. The same evil that existed long ago still exists today. People are still killing others, skill abusing and torturing others, and there is still a lot of suffering going on in the world. The only ways to stop this would be to stop doing the evil acts and to prevent the seeds of evil to start.

Rwanda

This was one of the most brutal modern genocide that took place in the small country of Rwanda in Africa. The method of killing people was that of a machete. People were literally hacked to death. It was also one of the strangest genocides to have taken place.

The country has only a couple of ethnic groups. The Hutu went after the Tutsi. At the time the Hutu were in control of the government and the military. There was a Tutsi rebel army that was in exile in a nearby country. The president was going to visit the rebels and his plane was shot down and he was killed. This sparked the government to promote people the Hutu to kill Tutsi all over the country.

In a bizarre course of events neighbors were killing neighbors. Within three months nearly a million people were slaughtered. It was only when the Tutsi army came into the country and took over that the killing of the Tutsi stopped. Many of the Hutu then fled the country out of fear of retaliation.

The only reason for this insane behavior was that many of the Hutu hated the Tutsi from being oppressed by an earlier regime. The words that were spread throughout the country were of hate on both sides. It was like how bullies at a school spark a number of fights. Imagine what you would do if the government told you to kill your neighbor.

Other Genocides

In Bosnia there were Muslims that were killed. The government did an ethnic cleansing of neighborhoods. It started when the former country of Yugoslavia broke up into several countries and left Bosnia with several ethnic groups that wanted power. It resulted in a civil war that lasted form 1992-1995. Thousands of people died most of them Bosniak Muslims.

During this time a village of 8,000 Bosniak Muslims were massacred and placed in a mass grave. This started with the seeds of hate from the Serbs who disliked the Bosnian Muslims. Throughout history there are areas of conflict when ethnic groups are thrown into the same area and they grow to dislike each other.

In Darfur an area in Sudan the Arab Sudanese attacked the Black Sudanese killing over 400,000 people and resulting in over a million displaced people. It is considered a genocide because it was racially targeted. The government ordered militia groups to go through villages killing Black Sudanese people. This again was sparked by racially or ethnically different people who disliked each other.

Refugees

It seems like there has always been people fleeing from their homes for safety. But in the 21st century it has been a crisis far beyond any in the past. there has been upwards of 25 million people who have fled their country so far. You see this all over Africa and the Middle East as countries are split up by civil war.

By far one of the worst has been in Syria. This is where it started with peaceful protests against the oppressive government, and turned into the government killing the protesters. Eventually the protesters got armed and started a civil war against the government.

The worst part of it was that there is not just two sides to the conflict. Several rebel groups started up being backed by many different countries. Each of the rebel groups is trying to take control of the country. ISIS the Islamic extremist group that wanted to create their own country with extremist ideas for running it is another group trying to gain power.

In other words Syria is a country that has been torn apart by several different groups and many of the innocent people have had enough and left the country. This has put millions of people in nearby countries like Lebanon, Jordan, and Turkey which has put a lot of strain on these countries. Many of the refugees have also fled to Europe to take refuge from the war. The implications of the refugee crisis will be felt for decades to come and could result in the destabilization of other countries and more wars.

Terrorism

The thing about terrorism that makes it so evil, is that it places fear in the hearts of people everywhere. This is why it is terrorism. If countries and people everywhere would just put terrorism in its place and didn't put so much emphasis on it. The terrorists would not have anywhere to advertise their handiwork. Many of them do it in order to get media coverage and let the world know they are here. There are many criminals that do the same thing, where they just want to have their three minutes of fame by committing a terrible crime.

Terrorism is fueled by people who get financial support to get weapons and then recruit young men who are generally out of work and want to belong to something. Terrorists will often use religion and twist its beliefs to fit their agenda so that they can gain power in a certain part of the world and get the world's attention.

People around the world then become afraid of terrorist acts in their neighborhoods so they start to become afraid of certain groups of people. This then turns into something more sinister with attacks on refugees or people of a certain religion. Terrorism creates more violence and death. Just think about all of the Afghanistan people who were killed after 9/11 terrorist attacks on the United States. It becomes an unending cycle of death.

Modern Slavery

Modern slavery comes in many forms. There are a lot of girls who are forced into prostitution. Some are kidnapped, others sold by parents, and some who fall into that lifestyle because they do not have anything else to do. It is a sad situation that often has an unhappy ending.

I lived in Chicago for a couple of years and hear a lot of sad stories. Young girls would run away from home and end up on the streets of Chicago. They would not have any place to go. Those who had a group of prostitutes would seek out and recruit these young girls. They would give them a place to stay some money. In return they would be trapped in an unpleasant situation with no where to turn.

Child soldiers is another common form of slavery. The same situation happens where they are kidnapped or recruited since they have no where else to go. Many of them are given drugs and indoctrinated into being killing machines. Several end up getting killed and many are mentally scared for the rest of their life.

Then there is the situation where many children and adults are trapped in working in sweat shops for several hours a day seven days a week without any benefits. Many of the work in unsafe conditions and get paid almost nothing. They continue to work there, because the alternative is not as pleasant. It is the owners of these factories who exploit the employees as they cut corners to make more money.

All of these forms of slavery were started and fueled by the same evil seeds that ran other forms of slavery throughout history. The main one is greed and the idea of making more money at the expense of someone else's freedom and happiness.

Pornography

Pornography is a big business. People get billions of dollars from pornography. It degrades those who are part of it. The industry prays of the addiction of others who pay to see it. It is just as addictive as any drug. Pornography has caused a lot of pain in the world and has broken up more families than anything else.

Pornography has also led to other more serious crimes like rape and exploitation of children.

People have taken something that is natural and has turned it into something ugly. This is one evil that can take even the best of society and destroy their lives. Just like how King David had been seduced by Bathsheba.

Organized Crime

The greatest evil in the 21st century is organized crime. Drug cartels and gangs are getting more powerful as they get money and buy modern weapons. Some of them are just as powerful as an army and are hard to contain. They commit all acts of evil and have the power to control a region of the world. If left unchecked these organization will be able to influence police and governments to the point that they are calling the shots and not the government officials.

There are groups of organized crime all over the world living in the shadows often just keeping out of the reach of the law. They meet in secret and do things in secret as not to draw attention to themselves unless they have enough power and then they don't care so much about people knowing what they have done. These people would make Hitler look like a saint. If they were able to gain some power and authority who knows what would happen. You do not want them pushing any buttons on nuclear devices.

Hate Groups

There are hate groups around the world. Just in the United States alone their are hundreds of hate groups who push their racist propaganda on others. The scary thing is that these groups are preparing for a day when they could take over and push their beliefs on others. They are waiting for the right time to act. Government officials have their eyes on these groups, but if there is a time when the country is involved in something else, or the government officials are sympathetic towards these groups they may do something unthinkable.

There have already been several encounters with police and government officials dealing with hate groups where people have been killed. The Oklahoma City bombing that killed 168 people in 1995. It was in response to an attack on a compound in Waco, Texas where a fanatical religious group was storing weapons. There was also the Ruby Ridge incident where some people were killed when government officials went to investigate a family who had weapons.

Some would say that American have the right to have guns because of the 2nd amendment of the constitution. I do not think that those who wrote the amendment thought that it included having weapons enough to create a small army and get ready to start a revolution as well as wipe out different ethnic groups.

The intent of these hate groups are far worse than people just getting prepared for emergencies and using weapons for hunting. The scary part is when these groups band together and start to target local law enforcement officers, or turn into terrorists and start to blow up buildings.

Chapter Six: Good vs. Evil

The good guy always wins in the movies. But in reality evil sometimes takes charge and causes a lot of damage, pain, and suffering for millions of people. When evil wins everyone loses. Those who commit the evil are no more happier about what they had done and are often tormented for it. In the end the people who commit evil acts die just like everyone else, but the evil they caused continues like a disease going from on corpse to the next. The victims of the evil suffer from the actions. They may be affected by these evil acts for many generations

Good Actions

It is the good actions of others that overcomes the evil. In the past evil may have had an impact on many people's lives, but it was the good that was done that made it so people had hope and were able to continue despite all of the evil around them. It is through the good that people do that allows humanity to survive. If it wasn't for the good in the world, evil would consume it.

Edmund Burke said, "All that is necessary for the triumph of evil is that good men do nothing." It is through good acts that we can hold back the tide of evil in the world today. This pattern has been repeated over and over again throughout history.

If we do not do good and act upon our good feelings and ideas evil will come into our hearts. Millions have died or suffered from the evil practices of others because people did nothing. Germany is a perfect example of a lot of good people doing nothing while their neighbors were taken away in camps. People throughout history have stood by and watched as people have been brutally slaughtered and tortured. Just think of all of the people who looked the other way as slaves were bought and sold as cattle.

There have been those who have trumped against the bad. William Wilberforce in the UK championed the cause for ending the slave trade and slavery in the British Empire. He was able to succeed and to pass through many social reforms in Britain before his death. Wilberforce along with several others in Britain was able to stop the evil of slavery without having a civil war.

In all of the genocides that have taken place their are stories of good people who have rescued people. During the Holocaust their was the entire people of Denmark who defied Hitler and helped Jewish people escape to freedom from the Nazis. Antonina Zabinski and her husband Dr. Jan Zabinski helped to save Polish Jews at the risk of their own lives. Oskar Schindler saved over a thousand Jewish people during the Holocaust, and there were many more people who helped to save people during the evil reign of the Nazis. We would not have the precious book of Anne Frank's Dairy if it wasn't for the family who helped her and her family from the Nazis.

During the Rwanda Genocide Paul Rusesabagina helped to save over a thousand people in the hotel he managed. There were also others who helped. It was through the good of many people that there were survivors who were able to tell their story to the world.

There are countless stories of those who were able to make a difference throughout history. Many people today are also doing good in the world. Malala Yousafzai through her actions has changed the world sees the treatment of girls in parts of the world where they are denied an education. Despite being shot in the head she still has a voice for good in the world.

Evil will never prevail when their is a voice for good in the world. This is one reason why people who do evil acts want to silence those who are good and who want good in the world. It is hard to silence an idea one that many people are born with. The idea is freewill and happiness.

Freewill and Happiness

Evil is about taking away freewill. In every case of evil it will take away people's freedom. There is slavery itself that takes away all human rights. There is murder that takes the life and the happiness of the loved ones. There is rape and pornography that takes away virtue and chastity. Every evil act is geared towards taking away happiness and freedom.

It is a person's ability to be happy and have the freedom to worship, to think, to express her feelings that brings about the good in the world. This does not mean people should infringe upon other people's freedoms or rights either. It is the rights given in the Declaration of Independence, the Constitution of the United States and the Declaration of Rights for the United Nations that says it all. If the world would just follow these human rights the world would be a better place and people would be happy.

Opposition

Despite our desire to have a world without hate, without fear, and one with continual good. There is an opposition that comes from people doing evil things. This is something that will continue in the future. It is natures way of showing us what is right and what is wrong. It is how we truly see what evil is. We do not have to seek out evil in its many forms, we can just see through evil eyes of the past and learn from the mistakes of the past.

Chapter Seven: Our Humanity

It is through our humanity that we can seek to do good in the world. It is only when we act inhuman that evil takes over. When men turn other women into objects of pleasure. When neighbor turns against neighbor and sees them as insects to exterminate. It is when a race of people is seen as inferior. It is when a religion is vilified. In all accounts of evil people are dehumanized into something that can be abused, slaughtered, or tortured.

Education

We must educate our children to be tolerant of religions, respectful of adults, parents, and the opposite sex, and to treat all people as equals. Through all of the years I have been teaching, I have seen the future. I have seen horrible children do horrible things. I have seen children who enjoy hurting others verbally and physically. At times I feel sick inside and a darkness thinking about what these children will turn out to be as adults.

I have also seen the hearts of children who are good inside. Those who have a sweat innocence about them. There are those who are extremely polite and willing to serve others. These children give me hope that the world will continue to move forward and their is just enough good in the world to overcome the evil influences of the world. It didn't take a lot of good people to defeat the Nazis and Hitler's final solution.

The power of non-violence brought about the freedom of millions in India, in the South, and in South Africa. The power of good acts captivate the hearts of people around the world. Evil will repel, good will attract. Babies respond to love and tenderness. Those same babies will grind, cry, and shy away from evil and harshness.

God dwells with the righteous, while the evil hides from God. All people were born with an innate power to do good. Even the worst among us can change and start to do good. The world needs to change. Men need to stand up and be counted as men take care of their families, stop the destructive effects of pornography, and give women the rights they deserve. Leaders of countries need to pass laws with the people of their countries in mind. They need to be able to work together with other countries to solve their humanitarian issues.

All people need to work together in harmony to solve the ills of the world and to resist the evil tendencies inside of them. People need to recognize what evil is and to act against it and work towards doing good.

Resources

Ackerman, Diane. *The Zookeeper's Wife*. W.W.
    Norton & Company, 2017.
Beah, Ishmael. *A Long Way Gone: Memoirs of a Boy
    Soldier*. Penguin, 2013.
Browning, Christopher R. *Ordinary Men: Reserve
    Police Battalion 101 and the Final Solution in
    Poland*. Harper Perennial, 2017.
Ilibagiza Immaculée, and Steve Erwin. *Left to Tell:
    One Woman's Story of Surviving the Rwandan
    Holocaust*. Hay House, 2014.
Keat, Nawuth & Kendall Martha. *Alive in the
    Killing Fields*. National Geographic, 2009.
Lower, Wendy. *Hitler's Furies: German Women in the
    Nazi Killing Fields*. Vintage Books, 2014.
Lowry, Lois. *Number the Stars*. Houghton Mifflin
    Harcourt, 2014.
Rusesabagina, Paul. *An Ordinary Man*. Bloomsbury
    Publishing, 2014.
Yousafzai, Malala, and Christina Lamb. *I Am Malala:
    the Girl Who Stood up for Education and Was
    Shot by the Taliban*. Weidenfeld &
    Nicolson, 2016.

* 9 7 8 1 9 7 7 8 2 2 1 9 2 *